JESUS LOVES YOU

Disclaimer Notice:

Every effort has been made to ensure the accuracy and integrity of the content provided. However, no guarantees of any kind are declared or implied.

Sources:

All Bible-derived content is drawn from the NIV, NLT, NASB, and NKJV translations.

Image Notice:

The cover image was created using AI technology and is for illustrative purposes only. All images in this book are symbolic and not meant to represent actual appearance. The images should not be taken as exact representations of products, services, or individuals, and no actual resemblance to any specific person or entity is intended or implied.

Contact Us:

✉ MyBibleWorkbooks@gmail.com

⧉ Projectkingdomcome

f Projectkingdomcome

PROJECT KINGDOM COME
ISBN 978-1-961786-15-8

Get The Entire Workbook Series!

THE BOOK OF
GENESIS
BIBLE-BASED WORKBOOK

Take an adventure into the amazing Book of Genesis
and test your knowledge as you go!

...male and female He created them. Genesis 1:27

PROJECT KINGDOM COME

THE BOOKS OF
EXODUS & JOSHUA
BIBLE-BASED WORKBOOK

Take an adventure into the amazing Books of Exodus and Joshua
and test your knowledge as you go!

Sun, stand still! Joshua 10:12

PROJECT KINGDOM COME

THE BOOKS OF
I & II SAMUEL
BIBLE-BASED WORKBOOK

Take an adventure into the amazing Books of 1st and 2nd Samuel
and test your knowledge as you go!

And they anointed David king over the house of Judah. 2nd Samuel 2:4

PROJECT KINGDOM COME

THE BOOKS OF
I & II KINGS
BIBLE-BASED WORKBOOK

Take an adventure into the amazing Books of 1st and 2nd Kings
and test your knowledge as you go!

and he shall come and sit on my throne and be king. 1st Kings 1:35

PROJECT KINGDOM COME

THE BOOKS OF
ESTHER & RUTH
BIBLE-BASED WORKBOOK

Take an adventure into the amazing Books of Esther and Ruth
and test your knowledge as you go!

And she obtained grace and favor in his sight. Esther 2:17

PROJECT KINGDOM COME

THE BOOKS OF
DANIEL & JOB
BIBLE-BASED WORKBOOK

Take an adventure into the amazing Books of Daniel and Job
and test your knowledge as you go!

they brought Daniel and threw him into the lions' den. Daniel 6:16

PROJECT KINGDOM COME

THE BOOK OF
MATTHEW
BIBLE-BASED WORKBOOK

Take an adventure into the amazing Book of Matthew
and test your knowledge as you go!

Behold, a virgin shall be with child. Matthew 1:23

PROJECT KINGDOM COME

THE BOOK OF
MARK
BIBLE-BASED WORKBOOK

Take an adventure into the amazing Book of Mark
and test your knowledge as you go!

Let us go into the next towns, that I may preach there also. Mark 1:38

PROJECT KINGDOM COME

THE BOOK OF
LUKE
BIBLE-BASED WORKBOOK

Take an adventure into the amazing Book of Luke
and test your knowledge as you go!

...there they crucified Him. Luke 23:33

PROJECT KINGDOM COME

THE BOOK OF
JOHN
BIBLE-BASED WORKBOOK

Take an adventure into the amazing Book of John
and test your knowledge as you go!

I am the resurrection and the life. John 11:25

PROJECT KINGDOM COME

THE BOOK OF
ACTS
BIBLE-BASED WORKBOOK

Take an adventure into the amazing Book of Acts
and test your knowledge as you go!

In the name of Jesus Christ of Nazareth, rise up and walk. Acts 3:6

PROJECT KINGDOM COME

THE BOOK OF
REVELATION
BIBLE-BASED WORKBOOK

Take an adventure into the amazing Book of Revelation
and test your knowledge as you go!

Look, He is coming with the clouds, and every eye will see Him. Revelation 1:7

PROJECT KINGDOM COME

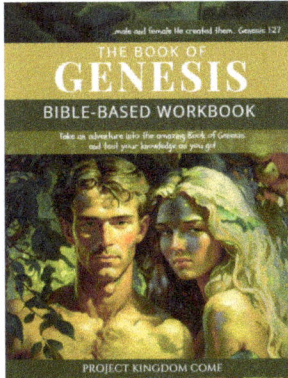

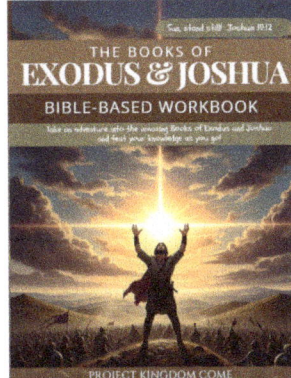

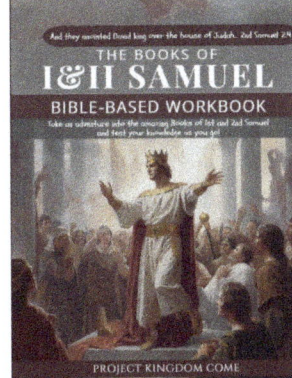

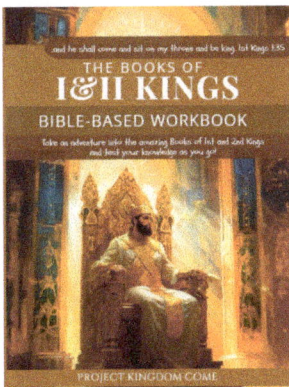

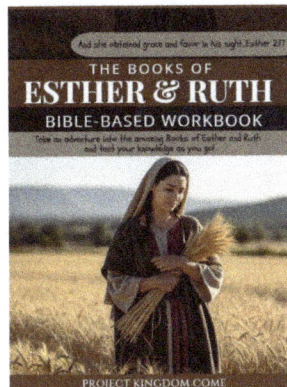

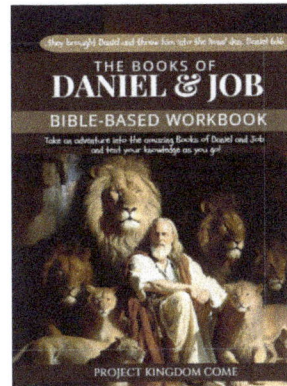

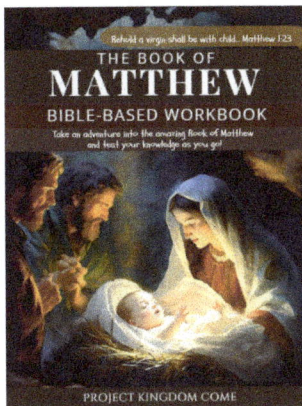

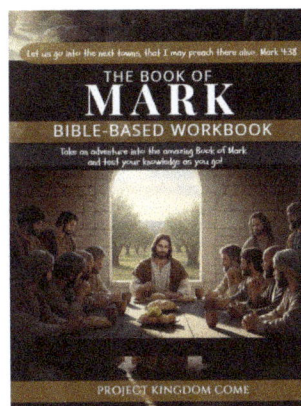

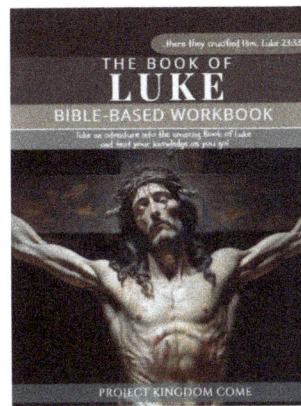

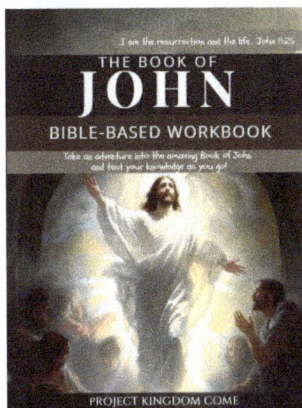

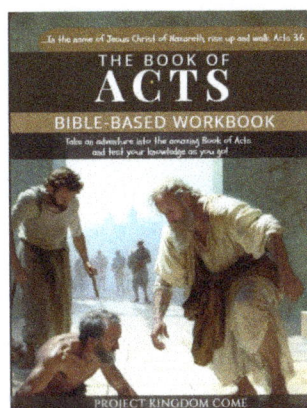

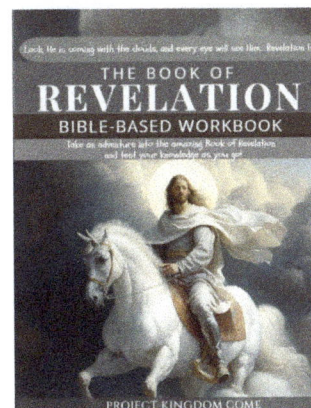

WWW.MYBIBLEWORKBOOKS.COM

PROJECT KINGDOM COME

This workbook belongs to:

_____

_____

_____

Leave your mark!

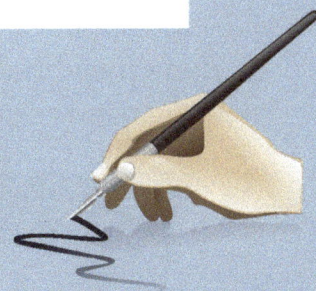

HOW TO USE THIS WORKBOOK

This workbook is designed to help young people explore the treasures in God's Word while having fun, growing in faith, and learning how to search the Scriptures for life's answers.

Here is what you will find inside:

Multiple Choice Questions

Each question comes directly from Scripture and includes a reference verse to help with locating the answer in the Bible. If possible, use a physical Bible to search for the answers.

Weekly Segments

Questions are grouped in weekly categories that could also be completed in a shorter or longer time frame.

Weekly Memory Verses

At the start of every week is a Bible verse to memorize. Each day of that week will repeat that memory verse with a chance to test memorization at the end of the week.

Certificate of Completion

At the end of the workbook, please find a Certificate of Achievement, ready for the child's name and parent or teacher's signature. Celebrate the accomplishment of studying an entire book in the Bible!

Answer Key

The workbook contains an answer key to serve as a support tool for parents or teachers reviewing the responses.

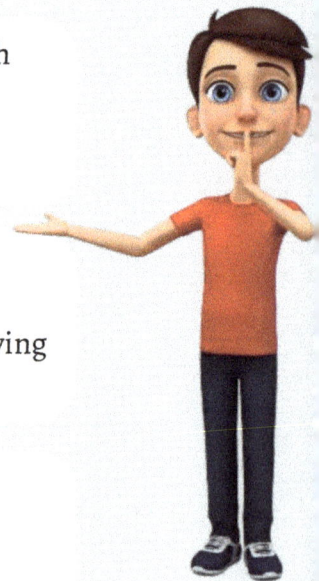

Recommendation for Parents and/or Teachers: Review the responses with your child or student and discuss lessons learned or interesting insights, to improve the child's retention and enrichment in the knowledge of God's word.

You can do all things through Christ who gives you strength!
Philippians 4:13

SAMPLE QUESTION...
HOW TO USE THIS WORKBOOK

> Reading the reference verse will always lead you to the correct **answer!**

In the beginning, God created: (Genesis 1:1)

(A) The Heavens and the Earth
B. Heaven and Earth
C. Heaven only
D. Earth only

> The number that comes after the book is the 'Chapter'

> This is the name of a book in the Bible

Joshua 1:8

> The number after the chapter is the 'Verse'

> NOW TEST YOURSELF! FIND JOSHUA CHAPTER 1 VERSE 8 IN YOUR BIBLE!

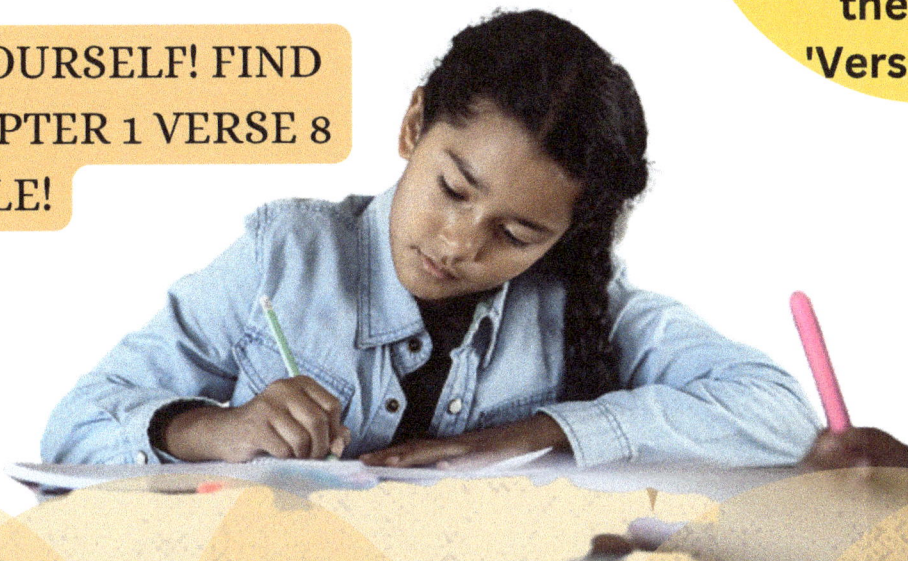

INTRODUCTION: THE BOOK OF 1ST SAMUEL

When God Calls You, Obedience Is Everything

The Book of **1 Samuel** is a powerful story of **prayer, leadership, and trusting God's voice.** It begins with the faithful cry of a woman named Hannah, and from her tears, a prophet is born. Samuel is called as a child to hear God's voice, speak His truth, and anoint kings for Israel.

As you journey through this book, you will meet King Saul, a man chosen by God, but who disobeyed and lost his place. And then comes David — a young shepherd boy, full of courage and faith, who is anointed to be king.

As you journey through 1 Samuel, you will discover:
- **God hears every prayer, even the silent ones**
- **Obedience is better than sacrifice**
- **God uses ordinary people to do extraordinary things**
- **Jealousy, pride, and fear can destroy a calling**
- **Victory comes not by sword or spear — but by the power of God!**

From battles to betrayals, worship to warfare, 1 Samuel teaches us how to **trust God's voice, wait on His timing, and walk in obedience,** even when it's hard.

If God is calling you to something greater — this book will help you answer with courage, obedience, and faith.

"Man looks at the outward appearance, but the Lord looks at the heart." - 1 Samuel 16:7

"The battle is the Lord's." - 1 Samuel 17:47

WEEK 1

1. What were the names of Elkanah's two wives? (1 Samuel 1: 1-2)

A. Naomi and Ruth
B. Sarah and Rebecca
C. Hannah and Peninnah
D. Hophni and Phineas

2. What positions did Hophni and Phinehas hold in Shiloh, and why was God displeased with them? (1 Samuel 1:3; 2:12-17)

A. They were prophets of the Lord who gave bad advice
B. They were priests who dishonored God and did evil in His sight
C. They were judges who failed to lead well
D. They were worship leaders who misled the people

WEEK 1 MEMORY VERSE: 1 SAMUEL 2:2
There is no one holy like the Lord; there is no one besides you; there is no Rock like our God.

WEEK 1

3. Which of the following is true about Elkanah's wives? (1 Samuel 1:2)

A. Peninnah had children, but Hannah had none
B. Sarah had children, but Rebekah had none
C. Hannah had children, but Peninnah had none
D. They were both from Egypt and worshiped idols

4. Why did Elkanah give Hannah a double portion of meat? (1 Samuel 1:5)

A. Because meat was her favorite food
B. Because she always cooked for the family
C. Because she had to share with her children
D. Because he loved her deeply, though the Lord had closed her womb

WEEK 1 MEMORY VERSE: 1 SAMUEL 2:2
There is no one holy like the Lord; there is no one besides you; there is no Rock like our God.

5. Why did Peninnah mock and provoke Hannah year after year? (1 Samuel 1:6-7)

A. Because Hannah had no children, and Peninnah wanted to make her miserable
B. Because Hannah was lazy and ungrateful
C. Because Peninnah was older and didn't want to be replaced
D. Because she wanted Hannah to stop praying

6. What vow did Hannah make if God gave her a son? (1 Samuel 1:11)

A. She would dedicate him to the Lord all his life
B. A razor would never touch his head
C. He would grow up in the palace
D. Both A and B are correct

WEEK 1 MEMORY VERSE: 1 SAMUEL 2:2
There is no one holy like the Lord; there is no one besides you;
there is no Rock like our God.

WEEK 1

7. **Why did Eli the priest think that Hannah was drunk? (1 Samuel 1:12-14)**

A. Because Hannah was crying loudly and uncontrollably
B. Because Hannah could not walk in a straight line
C. Because she was praying in her heart, and her lips were moving but no sound could be heard
D. Because she was eating meat in the temple

8. **What was the name of Hannah's firstborn son, given in answer to her prayers? (1 Samuel 1:20)**

A. Samuel
B. Joshua
C. Caleb
D. Moses

WEEK 1 MEMORY VERSE: 1 SAMUEL 2:2
There is no one holy like the Lord; there is no one besides you; there is no Rock like our God.

9. What does the Bible say not to do in 1 Samuel 2:3?

A. Do not speak with pride or let arrogance come from your mouth
B. Do not use curse words when talking to others
C. Do not speak when elders are speaking
D. Do not speak about things you do not understand

10. What was the problem with Eli's sons? (1 Samuel 2: 22-25)

A. They stole from the temple and people's homes
B. They slept with the women who served at the entrance of the Tent of Meeting, which was a very serious sin
C. They betrayed Prophet Samuel to the Philistines
D. They refused to learn how to offer sacrifices

WEEK 1 MEMORY VERSE: 1 SAMUEL 2:2
There is no one holy like the Lord; there is no one besides you; there is no Rock like our God.

WEEK 1

11. **What gift did Hannah bring Samuel each year when she visited him at the temple? (1 Samuel 2:19)**

A. Pictures of his family and a small kid-sized Bible
B. Animals to sacrifice to the Lord
C. Anointing oil and the Law of Moses
D. A little robe she had made for him

12. **After giving Samuel to God, how many more children did Hannah have? (1 Samuel 2:21)**

A. 7
B. 6
C. 5
D. 4

WEEK 1 MEMORY VERSE: 1 SAMUEL 2:2
There is no one holy like the Lord; there is no one besides you;
there is no Rock like our God.

13. Which of the following was expected of priests? (1 Samuel 2:28)

A. To go up to the Altar of God
B. To burn incense
C. To wear an ephod in God's presence
D. All the above

14. What did God say would happen to Eli's sons, Hophni and Phineas? (1 Samuel 2: 34)

A. They would be stoned outside the city
B. They would both die on the same day
C. They would become priests after their father Eli
D. They would train young Samuel

WEEK 1 MEMORY VERSE: 1 SAMUEL 2:2

There is no one holy like the Lord; there is no one besides you; there is no Rock like our God.

My heart rejoices in the Lord; my horn is exalted in the Lord
(1 Samuel 2:1)

Great job completing the week!

Did you memorize the daily verse?
Test yourself by writing it here...

_____

_____

_____

_____

_____

_____

Use this space to draw a scene from the Bible or reflect on something you learned, felt or experienced...

WEEK 2

15. How many times did Samuel hear a voice calling him before he realized it was the Lord? (1 Samuel 3:2-10)

A. 1

B. 2

C. 3

D. 4

16. Whose voice was calling Samuel in the night? (1 Samuel 3:8-10)

A. Eli the priest

B. Samuel's father

C. The Lord

D. Samuel's mother

WEEK 2 MEMORY VERSE: 1 SAMUEL 2:30B

Those who honor me I will honor, but those who despise me will be disdained.

17. Why did God judge Eli's household?
(1 Samuel 3:12-13)

A. Because they refused to teach Samuel the ways of God

B. Because Eli's sons blasphemed against God, Eli did not stop them.

C. Because his sons became farmers in Egypt

D. Because they touched the ark without permission

18. What does it mean that God did not let any of Samuel's words fall to the ground?
(1 Samuel 3: 19-20)

A. Everything Samuel spoke came to pass, because God established him

B. His words were remembered by Eli's sons

C. God gave Samuel visions and dreams instead of words

D. It means that the Lord made sure Samuel was unable to speak lies

WEEK 2 MEMORY VERSE: 1 SAMUEL 2:30B

Those who honor me I will honor, but those who despise me will be disdained.

WEEK 2

19. What happened when the Israelites fought the Philistines for the first time?
(1 Samuel 4:1-3)

A. The Philistines surrendered and begged for peace
B. The Israelites defeated the Philistines in battle
C. Israel was defeated by the Philistines
D. Fire came down from heaven and destroyed the Philistines

20. What other major events happened during the battle with the Philistines?
(1 Samuel 4:10-11)

A. God spoke from Mount Sinai
B. The ark of God was captured
C. Hophni and Phinehas died
D. Both B and C

WEEK 2 MEMORY VERSE: 1 SAMUEL 2:30B
Those who honor me I will honor, but those who despise me will be disdained.

<<<<< WEEK 2 >>>>>

21. What was Eli the priest's physical condition when Israel went to fight the Philistines? (1 Samuel 4:14-15)

A. He was 98 years old and blind

B. He was 90 years old and strong

C. He had lost his hearing and sight

D. He was 100 years old and sick in bed

22. What happened to Eli when he heard the ark of God had been captured? (1 Samuel 4:17-18)

A. He fell from his chair and broke his neck, for he was old and heavy

B. He made a sacrifice to ask for God's mercy

C. He rejected his priestly duties and mourned for his sons

D. He called Joshua to help recover the ark

WEEK 2 MEMORY VERSE: 1 SAMUEL 2:30B

Those who honor me I will honor, but those who despise me will be disdained.

23. What happened to Phinehas' wife when she heard about Eli and her husband's deaths? (1 Samuel 4:19-21)

A. She mourned for 40 days

B. She prayed in the temple

C. She gave birth to a son, named him Ichabod, and then she died

D. She ran away into the wilderness

24. What is the meaning of the name "Ichabod"? (1 Samuel 4: 21-22)

A. The Lord is strong and mighty

B. The glory of God has departed (left)

C. The Lord will provide

D. This far the Lord has brought us

WEEK 2 MEMORY VERSE: 1 SAMUEL 2:30B

Those who honor me I will honor, but those who despise me will be disdained.

WEEK 2

25. Where did the Philistines place the ark of God after capturing it? (1 Samuel 5:1-2)

A. In the king's palace

B. In the temple of Dagon, next to their god

C. In the city streets for everyone to see

D. On a mountain in Ashdod

26. What did the Philistines find had happened to Dagon on the first morning after placing him next to the ark? (1 Samuel 5:3)

A. Dagon had fallen face down before the ark of the Lord

B. Lightning had struck Dagon

C. Dagon had grown too large to fit in the temple

D. Dagon crumbled to dust at the sight of the ark

WEEK 2 MEMORY VERSE: 1 SAMUEL 2:30B

Those who honor me I will honor, but those who despise me will be disdained.

<<<<<< WEEK 2 >>>>>>

> **27. What happened to Dagon on the second day in the presence of the ark? (1 Samuel 5:4-5)**
>
> A. Dagon was stolen during the night
> B. Dagon disappeared
> C. Dagon fell again and broke his head and hands
> D. The ark was glowing brightly

> **28. What happened to the Philistines in every town where they took the ark? (1 Samuel 5:6-10)**
>
> A. They were blessed with riches
> B. They turned from idols and worshiped God
> C. They were struck with tumors and fear
> D. They carried on as if nothing happened

WEEK 2 MEMORY VERSE: 1 SAMUEL 2:30B

Those who honor me I will honor, but those who despise me will be disdained.

Because I honor the Lord,
He will honor me
(1 Samuel 2:30b)

Great job completing the week!

Did you memorize the daily verse?
Test yourself by writing it here...

_____

_____

_____

_____

_____

_____

Use this space to draw a scene from the Bible or reflect on something you learned, felt or experienced...

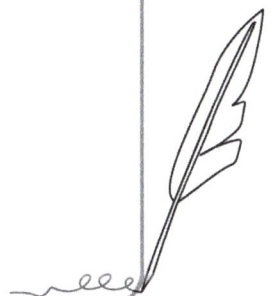

> **29. Which group of Philistines refused to keep the ark in their town? (1 Samuel 5:10-11)**
>
> A. The people of Ashdod
> B. The people of Ebenezer
> C. The people of Gath
> D. The people of Ekron

> **30. How long did the Philistines keep the ark of God before returning it?**
> **(1 Samuel 6:1-2)**
>
> A. 1 week
> B. 7 months
> C. 12 months
> D. 40 years

WEEK 3 MEMORY VERSE: 1 SAMUEL 15:22

Does the Lord delight in burnt offerings and sacrifices as much as in obeying the Lord? To obey is better than sacrifice, and to heed is better than the fat of rams.

31. What guilt offering did the Philistines send with the ark of God when they returned it? (1 Samuel 6:3-5)

A. Anointing oil and spices

B. 5 cows and 5 lambs

C. 7 bags of silver and 7 bags of gold

D. 5 gold tumors and 5 gold rats

32. How did the Philistines return the ark of God to Israel? (1 Samuel 6:7-9)

A. Using a cart pulled by two cows

B. On a royal chariot drawn by horses

C. Carried by servants on their backs

D. They attached poles to the sides of the ark and carried it

WEEK 3 MEMORY VERSE: 1 SAMUEL 15:22

Does the Lord delight in burnt offerings and sacrifices as much as in obeying the Lord? To obey is better than sacrifice, and to heed is better than the fat of rams.

33. What did the Levites do when the ark arrived in Beth Shemesh? (1 Samuel 6:13-15)

A. Sent it back to Samuel and asked God for mercy
B. Called the people to fast and pray
C. Burned the cart's wood and offered the cows as a sacrifice to the Lord
D. Refused to touch it and left it outside the city

34. Why did God strike down 70 people in Beth Shemesh? (1 Samuel 6:19)

A. Because they touched the ark
B. Because they looked into the ark, which was forbidden
C. Because they removed the ark's cover without permission
D. Because they refused to give a sacrifice

WEEK 3 MEMORY VERSE: 1 SAMUEL 15:22
Does the Lord delight in burnt offerings and sacrifices as much as in obeying the Lord? To obey is better than sacrifice, and to heed is better than the fat of rams.

35. How long did the ark remain in Kiriath Jearim? (1 Samuel 7:1-2)

A. 10 years

B. 20 years

C. 15 years

D. 40 years

36. What did Samuel tell the Israelites to do if they wanted to return to the Lord with all their hearts? (1 Samuel 7:3)

A. Get rid of all foreign gods and Ashtoreths

B. Commit to the Lord and serve Him only

C. All the above

D. None of the above

WEEK 3 MEMORY VERSE: 1 SAMUEL 15:22

Does the Lord delight in burnt offerings and sacrifices as much as in obeying the Lord? To obey is better than sacrifice, and to heed is better than the fat of rams.

37. What did the Philistines do when they heard the Israelites were gathering at Mizpah to pray? (1 Samuel 7:7)

A. Sent their prayer requests
B. Offered them 1,000 fat cows
C. Sent Goliath to fight them
D. Came up to attack them

38. Samuel named a stone "Ebenezer." What does Ebenezer mean? (1 Samuel 7:12)

A. The Philistines have been defeated
B. This far the Lord has helped us
C. God is our provider
D. God is our healer

WEEK 3 MEMORY VERSE: 1 SAMUEL 15:22
Does the Lord delight in burnt offerings and sacrifices as much as in obeying the Lord? To obey is better than sacrifice, and to heed is better than the fat of rams.

39. Why did the Israelites ask for a king?
(1 Samuel 8:4-5, 19-20)

A. Samuel was old, and his sons were corrupt
B. They wanted to be like other nations
C. They didn't want to be led by prophets anymore
D. Both A and B

40. What was Saul doing before Samuel anointed him king? (1 Samuel 9:3-4, 20)

A. Taking care of his father's sheep
B. Looking for his father's lost donkeys
C. Cooking soup for his father
D. Helping build his father's house

WEEK 3 MEMORY VERSE: 1 SAMUEL 15:22

Does the Lord delight in burnt offerings and sacrifices as much as in obeying the Lord? To obey is better than sacrifice, and to heed is better than the fat of rams.

41. How did Samuel anoint Saul to become king of Israel? (1 Samuel 10:1)

A. He asked the servants to lift Saul and parade him

B. Saul rode into town on a donkey

C. Samuel poured a flask of oil on Saul's head

D. Saul killed Goliath, and Samuel made him king

42. What happened to Saul when he met with a group of prophets? (1 Samuel 10:5-6)

A. The Spirit of the Lord came upon him, and he prophesied

B. He asked them for help finding his father's donkeys

C. He decided to live with them

D. Nothing happened to Saul

WEEK 3 MEMORY VERSE: 1 SAMUEL 15:22

Does the Lord delight in burnt offerings and sacrifices as much as in obeying the Lord? To obey is better than sacrifice, and to heed is better than the fat of rams.

I choose to obey God. My obedience
is my worship
(1 Samuel 15:22)

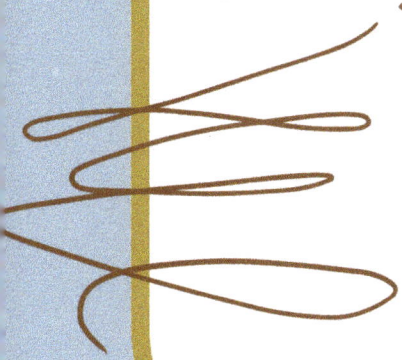

Great job completing the week!

Did you memorize the daily verse?
Test yourself by writing it here...

Use this space to draw a scene from the Bible or reflect on something you learned, felt or experienced...

43. What did Saul do when Samuel was ready to present him as king to the people?
(1 Samuel 10:20–23)

A. He put on royal clothes

B. He asked his father to walk him in

C. He was so afraid he hid among the supplies

D. He forgot to clean himself up

44. What did Samuel ask God to send as a sign during his speech to the people?
(1 Samuel 12:16–18)

A. Saul's lost donkeys

B. The sun and moon to stand still

C. Thunder and rain

D. A voice from heaven

WEEK 4 MEMORY VERSE: 1 SAMUEL 16:7B
For the Lord does not see as man sees; for man looks at the outward appearance, but the Lord looks at the heart.

45. According to 1 Samuel 12:20–21, what does Samuel tell the people?

A. Do not be afraid; even though you've done wrong, serve the Lord with all your heart and don't turn to useless idols

B. Stop serving the Lord and follow the gods of other nations

C. Offer more sacrifices so that God will forgive your sins

D. Ask Samuel to keep praying for you so you don't have to

46. How old was Saul when he became King? (1 Samuel 13: 1)

A. 17 years old

B. 30 years old

C. 33 years old

D. 18 years old

WEEK 4 MEMORY VERSE: 1 SAMUEL 16:7B
For the Lord does not see as man sees; for man looks at the outward appearance, but the Lord looks at the heart.

47. Why did Saul offer the sacrifice instead of waiting for Samuel? (1 Samuel 13:7–14)

A. Samuel was old and needed help

B. Samuel had not arrived by the seventh day

C. Saul wanted a blessing for wisdom

D. Saul was curious about how sacrifices worked

48. What did Jonathan eat after Saul told everyone not to eat anything? (1 Samuel 14:24–27)

A. Rice

B. Strawberries

C. Honey

D. Bananas

WEEK 4 MEMORY VERSE: 1 SAMUEL 16:7B

For the Lord does not see as man sees; for man looks at the outward appearance, but the Lord looks at the heart.

49. How did Saul disobey God's command concerning the Amalekites? (1 Samuel 15:2, 7–10)

A. He made peace with the Amalekites instead of fighting them

B. He destroyed the Amalekites but also destroyed Israel's altars

C. He refused to go into battle and hid from the Amalekites

D. He spared King Agag and kept the best animals instead of destroying everything

50. What happened after Saul disobeyed God's command? (1 Samuel 15:23)

A. God rejected Saul as king of Israel

B. Saul cried for 7 days and refused to eat

C. Saul asked God to make Jonathan king

D. Saul returned to caring for his father's donkeys

WEEK 4 MEMORY VERSE: 1 SAMUEL 16:7B
For the Lord does not see as man sees; for man looks at the outward appearance, but the Lord looks at the heart.

"

51. What truth is revealed in 1 Samuel 15:22-23?

A. Obeying God is more important than offering sacrifices

B. Rebellion is like the sin of witchcraft

C. Arrogance is like the sin of idolatry

D. All the above are correct

"

52. What does 1 Samuel 16:7 teach us about how God sees people?

A. The Lord doesn't look at what people see

B. People look at appearance, but God looks at the heart

C. Both A and B are correct

D. God only blesses those who look beautiful or strong

WEEK 4 MEMORY VERSE: 1 SAMUEL 16:7B
For the Lord does not see as man sees; for man looks at the outward appearance, but the Lord looks at the heart.

53. Who did God choose to be king after Saul? (1 Samuel 16:13)

A. David

B. Solomon

C. Jonathan

D. Jesus

54. What happened when Samuel anointed David to become king? (1 Samuel 16:13)

A. The Spirit of the Lord came upon him powerfully

B. He refused the anointing

C. His brothers laughed at him

D. He ran away and hid

WEEK 4 MEMORY VERSE: 1 SAMUEL 16:7B

For the Lord does not see as man sees; for man looks at the outward appearance, but the Lord looks at the heart.

55. What did Samuel use to anoint David as king? (1 Samuel 16:13)

A. Water

B. Oil

C. Salt

D. A jar of sand from Bethlehem

56. What was the name of the Philistine giant who fought against Israel? (1 Samuel 17:4)

A. Anakim

B. Saul

C. Goliath

D. Nimrod

WEEK 4 MEMORY VERSE: 1 SAMUEL 16:7B

For the Lord does not see as man sees; for man looks at the outward appearance, but the Lord looks at the heart.

Create in me a clean heart, O God,
and renew a right spirit
within me
(Psalm 51:10)

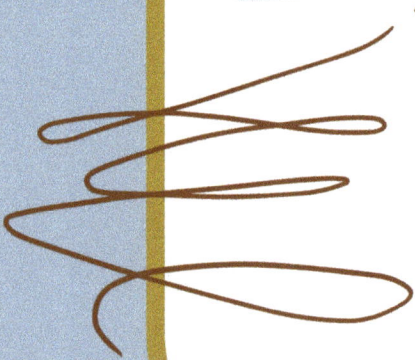

Great job completing the week!

Did you memorize the daily verse?
Test yourself by writing it here...

_____

_____

_____

_____

_____

Use this space to draw a scene from the Bible or reflect on something you learned, felt or experienced...

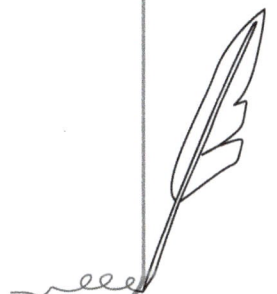

57. How many days did Goliath come out to challenge Israel's army? (1 Samuel 17:16)

A. 5 days

B. 25 days

C. 60 days

D. 40 days

58. What rewards were promised to the man who killed Goliath? (1 Samuel 17:25)

A. Great riches

B. The king's daughter in marriage

C. His family would not pay taxes

D. All the above

WEEK 5 MEMORY VERSE: 1 SAMUEL 17: 45B

You come to me with a sword, with a spear, and with a javelin. But I come to you in the name of the Lord of hosts, the God of the armies of Israel, whom you have defied.

59. What two animals had David killed while caring for his father's sheep?
(1 Samuel 17:34-36)

A. A lion and a crocodile

B. A lion and a bear

C. A bear and a tiger

D. A hippo and a lion

60. What does 1 Samuel 17:47 teach about how we win our battles?

A. The Lord saves not by sword or spear — the battle belongs to Him

B. God will help, but we must do most of the work

C. Swords and spears are the best way to fight

D. The battle goes to the strongest army

WEEK 5 MEMORY VERSE: 1 SAMUEL 17: 45B

You come to me with a sword, with a spear, and with a javelin. But I come to you in the name of the Lord of hosts, the God of the armies of Israel, whom you have defied.

61. What did David use to defeat Goliath?
(1 Samuel 17:48-50)

A. A sword
B. A gun
C. A sling and stone
D. Fire and a sword

62. Which of Saul's sons loved David deeply and became his best friend? (1 Samuel 18:1-3)

A. Abinadab
B. Jonathan
C. Malachi
D. Joseph

WEEK 5 MEMORY VERSE: 1 SAMUEL 17: 45B
You come to me with a sword, with a spear, and with a javelin. But I come to you in the name of the Lord of hosts, the God of the armies of Israel, whom you have defied.

63. Why did Saul become angry and jealous of David? (1 Samuel 18:7-9)

A. David was very handsome

B. David became close to Jonathan

C. Women sang that David had killed more enemies than Saul

D. David bragged about being stronger than Saul

64. What was the name of Saul's daughter who became David's wife? (1 Samuel 18:27)

A. Merab

B. Adriel

C. Deborah

D. Michal

WEEK 5 MEMORY VERSE: 1 SAMUEL 17: 45B

You come to me with a sword, with a spear, and with a javelin. But I come to you in the name of the Lord of hosts, the God of the armies of Israel, whom you have defied.

"

65. How did Saul try to kill David when an evil spirit came upon him while David was playing the harp? (1 Samuel 19:9-10)

A. He threw a spear at David

B. He took a sword and chased him

C. He threw him in a lion's den

D. He sent his army to arrest him

"

66. What strange thing did David do to protect himself when he was afraid of King Achish? (1 Samuel 21:10-13)

A. He acted like a madman

B. He scratched the doors and drooled

C. He let saliva run down his beard

D. All the above

WEEK 5 MEMORY VERSE: 1 SAMUEL 17: 45B

You come to me with a sword, with a spear, and with a javelin. But I come to you in the name of the Lord of hosts, the God of the armies of Israel, whom you have defied.

67. Where did David go to hide after leaving Gath? (1 Samuel 22:1)

A. The mountains of Jerusalem
B. The Cave of Adullam
C. The Cave of Gath
D. The Valley of Moab

68. How many men joined David while he was in hiding? (1 Samuel 22:2)

A. 100 men
B. 20 men
C. 400 men
D. 50 men

WEEK 5 MEMORY VERSE: 1 SAMUEL 17: 45B

You come to me with a sword, with a spear, and with a javelin. But I come to you in the name of the Lord of hosts, the God of the armies of Israel, whom you have defied.

"

69. What happened when Saul commanded his guards to kill the priests of the Lord?
(1 Samuel 22:17-18)

A. The guards obeyed and killed them

B. Doeg the Edomite killed them when the guards refused

C. The priests escaped into the wilderness

D. The guards arrested them without killing

"

70. Why didn't David kill Saul when he had the chance? (1 Samuel 24:9-11)

A. He didn't want to upset Jonathan

B. He only cut off a piece of Saul's robe and spared him

C. He refused to harm the Lord's anointed

D. Both B and C

WEEK 5 MEMORY VERSE: 1 SAMUEL 17: 45B

You come to me with a sword, with a spear, and with a javelin. But I come to you in the name of the Lord of hosts, the God of the armies of Israel, whom you have defied.

The Lord fights for me not by sword or spear. The battle belongs to Him!
(1 Samuel 17:47)

Great job completing the week!

Did you memorize the daily verse?
Test yourself by writing it here...

_____

_____

_____

_____

_____

Use this space to draw a scene from the Bible or reflect on something you learned, felt or experienced...

WEEK 6

> **71. What happened to Nabal after he refused to help David and his men? (1 Samuel 25:36–42)**
>
> A. He joined Saul's army to fight David
> B. He lost all his sheep and goats in the wilderness
> C. Nabal died, and David married his wife Abigail
> D. His wife ran away and refused to live with him

> **72. What did Saul do with Michal, David's wife? (1 Samuel 25:44)**
>
> A. She died in battle
> B. She cried daily for David
> C. He gave her to another man named Paltiel
> D. She stayed at home while David was in hiding

WEEK 6 MEMORY VERSE: 1 SAMUEL 30:6B
But David strengthened himself in the Lord his God.

73. What group helped Saul try to hunt down David? (1 Samuel 26:1)

A. The Moabites
B. The Perizzites
C. The Ziphites
D. The Jebusites

74. What did David do during his second chance to kill Saul? (1 Samuel 26:6–12)

A. He entered Saul's camp while everyone slept
B. He took Saul's spear and water jug
C. He did not harm Saul
D. All the above answers are correct

WEEK 6 MEMORY VERSE: 1 SAMUEL 30:6B
But David strengthened himself in the Lord his God.

75. How long did David live in Ziklag among the Philistines? (1 Samuel 27:6–7)

A. Two and a half years
B. 30 years
C. About one year
D. One year and four months

76. What did Saul do when he couldn't hear from God through dreams, Urim, or prophets? (1 Samuel 28:5–8)

A. He fasted and prayed until God answered
B. He did whatever he wanted
C. He went to a medium (a person claiming to be in contact with the spirits of the dead and to communicate between the dead and the living)
D. He asked a woman to help him fight the Philistines

WEEK 6 MEMORY VERSE: 1 SAMUEL 30:6B
But David strengthened himself in the Lord his God.

77. It is against God's will to speak with the spirits of dead people. Whose dead spirit did Saul ask the medium of Endor to call? (1 Samuel 28:8-11)

A. Abraham
B. Moses
C. Samuel
D. Job

78. What message did the spirit of Samuel give to Saul? (1 Samuel 28:16–19)

A. "The Lord has forgiven you"
B. "Offer a sacrifice and be restored"
C. "Tomorrow you and your sons will be with me"
D. "You will be king again in 7 years"

WEEK 6 MEMORY VERSE: 1 SAMUEL 30:6B
But David strengthened himself in the Lord his God.

79. What happened when David and his men went after the Amalekites who had raided Ziklag? (1 Samuel 30:17–19)

A. They were too afraid and fled
B. David recovered everything that was taken
C. The Amalekites destroyed the camp and all belongings
D. The Amalekites refused to return anything

80. What did David do with the plunder he took back from the Amalekites? (1 Samuel 30:26–30)

A. Burned it all
B. Gave it to his army and kept double
C. Left it behind
D. Gave it as gifts to friends and allies

WEEK 6 MEMORY VERSE: 1 SAMUEL 30:6B
But David strengthened himself in the Lord his God.

81. How did King Saul die?
(1 Samuel 31:4)

A. He was trampled by horses
B. He was wounded by arrows and died in hiding
C. He fell on his own sword
D. His son killed him accidentally

82. How many of Saul's sons died with him in battle? **(1 Samuel 31:6)**

A. 1
B. 2
C. 3
D. 4

WEEK 6 MEMORY VERSE: 1 SAMUEL 30:6B
But David strengthened himself in the Lord his God.

WEEK 6

83. How did David find out that King Saul and his son Jonathan had died? (2 Samuel 1:1–4)

A. The Lord sent an angel to inform David

B. A man escaped from the battle and came to tell David

C. One of David's men had gone to the war and came back with the news

D. David found King Saul and Jonathan lying on the battleground

84. . In what book is the song written that David taught the people to mourn for Saul and Jonathan? (2 Samuel 1:17-18)

A. The book of Exodus

B. The book of Enoch

C. The book of Jasher

D. The book of Revelation

WEEK 6 MEMORY VERSE: 1 SAMUEL 30:6B

But David strengthened himself in the Lord his God.

INTRODUCTION: THE BOOK OF 2ND SAMUEL

When God Lifts You, Remain Humble and Obedient

The Book of **2 Samuel** tells the incredible story of David — a man after God's own heart, as he rises to the throne and leads Israel as king. It is a book full of victories, worship, mistakes, and mercy. Through David's life, we see what it means to be chosen, anointed, and held accountable by God.

David defeats giants, unites a nation, brings back the ark of God, and leads his people in worship. But even mighty men fall. David makes a terrible mistake, yet he doesn't run from God, he runs to Him in repentance.

As you journey through 2 Samuel, you will discover:

- **Leadership is a gift and a responsibility**
- **God honors worship that comes from the heart**
- **Sin has consequences, but repentance brings restoration**
- **God's mercy is greater than our biggest failures**
- **God's promises never fail, even when we do**

This book reminds us that no matter how high God lifts us, we must stay humble, walk in obedience, and always return to Him when we fall.

If you've ever made a mistake, or needed a second chance, David's story will show you that God still writes beautiful stories with broken people.

"Create in me a clean heart, O God, and renew a steadfast spirit within me." — Psalm 51:10
"The Lord has established him as king over Israel... for the Lord was with him." — 2 Samuel 5:12

When I feel weak, I strengthen myself in the Lord my God! (1 Samuel 30:6)

Great job completing the week!

Did you memorize the daily verse?
Test yourself by writing it here...

_____

_____

_____

_____

_____

Use this space to draw a scene from the Bible or reflect on something you learned, felt or experienced...

WEEK 7

85. **Who did David move with to Hebron?**
 (2 Samuel 2:1-3)

A. His wife Ahinoam of Jezreel
B. His wife Abigail, the widow of Nabal
C. The men who were with him and their families
D. All the above

86. **What happened during the war between the house of Saul and the house of David?**
(2 Samuel 3:1)

A. David grew stronger and stronger while the house of Saul grew weaker and weaker
B. The house of Saul grew stronger and stronger while David grew weaker and weaker
C. Some men from Saul's army joined David's army
D. There was no war between David and the house of Saul

WEEK 7 MEMORY VERSE: 2 SAMUEL 22:29
You, LORD, are my lamp; the LORD turns my darkness into light.

WEEK 7

87. What did David ask for from Abner, before he agreed to work with him? (2 Samuel 3:12-14)

A. David asked Abner to bring Saul's sword
B. David asked that his wife Michal be given back to him
C. David asked that his son Absalom be made the commander of the army
D. David asked for 100 cows and sheep

88. What did Paltiel do when his wife was taken away from him? (2 Samuel 3:14-16)

A. He packed all his things and moved to Judah
B. He went and married two other wives
C. He went weeping and crying behind her all the way to Bahurim
D. He tried to stop her from leaving but was ordered to go back

WEEK 7 MEMORY VERSE: 2 SAMUEL 22:29

You, LORD, are my lamp; the LORD turns my darkness into light.

WEEK 7

89. When King David conquered the city of Jerusalem from the Jebusites, what new name did he give the city? (2 Samuel 5:6-9)

A. The City of Zion
B. The City of God
C. The City of David
D. The New Jerusalem

90. Who sent people and materials to build a palace for King David? (2 Samuel 5:11-12)

A. Hiram King of Tyre
B. Abraham
C. The Jebusites
D. Samuel the priest

WEEK 7 MEMORY VERSE: 2 SAMUEL 22:29

You, LORD, are my lamp; the LORD turns my darkness into light.

WEEK 7

91. What did King David do before he went to battle with the Philistines? (2 Samuel 5:18-19)

A. He took 300 strong men and prepared them for battle

B. He first asked the Lord whether he should go to attack the Philistines

C. He fasted for 3 days and 3 nights

D. He sent spies to study the Philistines

92. What is the meaning of 'Baal Perazim'? (2 Samuel 5:20)

A. As waters break out, the Lord has broken out against my enemies before me

B. The Philistines are mighty and win every battle

C. Baal lives in a Perazim

D. King Perazim is great

WEEK 7 MEMORY VERSE: 2 SAMUEL 22:29

You, LORD, are my lamp; the LORD turns my darkness into light.

WEEK 7

> 93. How many young men did David gather in order to bring the ark of God to Jerusalem? (2 Samuel 6:1-2)

A. 30
B. 300
C. 3000
D. 30,000

> 94. What did David and the people of Israel use to carry the ark of God? (2 Samuel 6:3)

A. Their shoulders
B. A new cart
C. The priests carried it as commanded in the Law
D. Abinadab himself carried it

WEEK 7 MEMORY VERSE: 2 SAMUEL 22:29

You, LORD, are my lamp; the LORD turns my darkness into light.

WEEK 7

95. Why did Uzzah reach out his hand to touch the ark of God? (2 Samuel 6:6-7)

A. Because the oxen carrying it stumbled, and the ark almost fell

B. Because he wanted to see how it felt to touch the ark

C. Because he wanted to take it home

D. Because it was too heavy for David to carry alone

96. What happened to Uzzah when he touched the ark of God? (2 Samuel 6:7)

A. He was struck with a skin disease and sent away

B. The ark disappeared, and Uzzah was afraid

C. Uzzah became rich and had many pieces of gold and silver

D. The Lord's anger struck him, and he died there

WEEK 7 MEMORY VERSE: 2 SAMUEL 22:29
You, LORD, are my lamp; the LORD turns my darkness into light.

WEEK 7

> 97. **When David saw what had happened to Uzzah, what did he do? (2 Samuel 6:8-11)**
>
> A. He was angry because of what happened
> B. David was afraid of the Lord and was not willing to take the ark to the City of David
> C. David left the ark in the house of Obed-Edom for 3 months
> D. All the above

> 98. **What happened to Obed-Edom? (2 Samuel 6:11-12)**
>
> A. He built a wooden house to store the ark of God
> B. He was afraid of the ark and refused to keep it in his house
> C. God blessed him and his home because of the ark
> D. Obed-Edom and his children were sick for 3 months

WEEK 7 MEMORY VERSE: 2 SAMUEL 22:29

You, LORD, are my lamp; the LORD turns my darkness into light.

God is my refuge and my strength, a very present help in times of trouble (Psalm 46:1)

Great job completing the week!

Did you memorize the daily verse?
Test yourself by writing it here...

_____

_____

_____

_____

_____

Use this space to draw a scene from the Bible or reflect on something you learned, felt or experienced...

99. How many children did David's wife Michal have? (2 Samuel 6:23)

A. 2 sons and 2 daughters
B. 1 son who was lame in both feet
C. She had no children
D. 4 daughters and no sons

100. What did David pray and say about the Lord in 2 Samuel 7:28?

A. Sovereign Lord, you are God!
B. The Lord's covenant (promise) is trustworthy
C. The Lord has promised good things to His servant
D. All the above

WEEK 8 MEMORY VERSE: 2 SAMUEL 22:31
As for God, His way is perfect; The word of the Lord is proven;
He is a shield to all who trust in Him.

101. What unusual method did David use to decide which Moabites would live or die after defeating them? (2 Samuel 8:2)

A. He had them drink water, and only those who licked with their tongues were spared

B. He made them line up to be judged by his soldiers

C. He measured them with a rope, and only some were allowed to live

D. He gave them heavy weapons, and only the strongest were kept alive

102. What did David do with all the gold, silver, and bronze that he got from his enemies? (2 Samuel 8:9–12)

A. He dedicated all of it to the Lord

B. He made jewelry for his daughters

C. He used it to make weapons for war

D. He gave it back to them and asked them to burn it

WEEK 8 MEMORY VERSE: 2 SAMUEL 22:31
As for God, His way is perfect; The word of the Lord is proven;
He is a shield to all who trust in Him.

103. Who was Mephibosheth?
(2 Samuel 9:3)

A. He was David's son with his wife Michal

B. He was the son of Jonathan, and he was lame in both feet

C. He was the son of Saul and was commander of the army

D. He was the king of the Ammonites

104. How did King David show kindness to Mephibosheth? (2 Samuel 9:6-7)

A. He gave him back all the land that belonged to his grandfather Saul

B. He invited him to always eat at the same table with David

C. Both A and B are correct

D. None of the above

WEEK 8 MEMORY VERSE: 2 SAMUEL 22:31
As for God, His way is perfect; The word of the Lord is proven;
He is a shield to all who trust in Him.

105. What is the name of the woman that David saw from the roof of his palace?
(2 Samuel 11:2-3)

A. Rebecca

B. Michal

C. Bethesda

D. Bathsheba

106. Who was Uriah the Hittite?
(2 Samuel 11:3)

A. He was Rebecca's husband

B. He was David's butler

C. He was Bathsheba's husband

D. He was a soldier in David's army

WEEK 8 MEMORY VERSE: 2 SAMUEL 22:31
As for God, His way is perfect; The word of the Lord is proven;
He is a shield to all who trust in Him.

107. What did David plan to do to Uriah in his letter to Joab? (2 Samuel 11:14-15)

A. He wanted Uriah to be made the king of Jerusalem

B. He planned to have Uriah killed at war

C. He wanted to keep Uriah from losing his job

D. He wanted Joab to make Uriah commander of David's army

108. Why was God not pleased with the things that David did? (2 Samuel 11: 14-15 & 27)

A. Because David had Uriah killed and then took his wife

B. Because David was supposed to help Uriah keep his job, but he did not

C. Because David was not going to war

D. Because David was praying to idols

WEEK 8 MEMORY VERSE: 2 SAMUEL 22:31
As for God, His way is perfect; The word of the Lord is proven;
He is a shield to all who trust in Him.

≪≪≪≪ WEEK 8 ≫≫≫≫

109. In Nathan's story to David, what did the rich man do to the poor man? (2 Samuel 12:1-4)

A. The rich man refused to give the poor man a place to sleep
B. The rich man took the poor man's wife
C. The rich man took the poor man's lamb
D. The rich man begged the poor man for water

110. What happened to David's first child with Uriah's widow? (2 Samuel 12:15-18)

A. He grew up to become a king
B. He was called Solomon
C. He was cared for by servants until he recovered
D. He became sick and died

WEEK 8 MEMORY VERSE: 2 SAMUEL 22:31
As for God, His way is perfect; The word of the Lord is proven;
He is a shield to all who trust in Him.

111. What did David do when he found out what had happened to the son he had with Bathsheba? (2 Samuel 12: 19-20)

A. He got up from the ground, stopped fasting and worshiped God, then went to his house to eat

B. He commanded the army to go fight his enemies in all of Israel

C. He decided that his son would go for training to become a king

D. He went on to fast for 7 more days

112. Why did the Lord send Nathan the prophet to give a new name to David's son? (2 Samuel 12:24-25)

A. Because the Lord loved him and named him Jedidiah

B. Because he was tall and handsome, the Lord named him Solomon

C. Because he was going to be a prophet, the Lord named him Absalom

D. The Lord named him David junior, because he was just like his father

WEEK 8 MEMORY VERSE: 2 SAMUEL 22:31
As for God, His way is perfect; The word of the Lord is proven; He is a shield to all who trust in Him.

"Some trust in chariots and some in horses, but I trust in the name of the Lord my God."
(Psalm 20:7)

Great job completing the week!

Did you memorize the daily verse?
Test yourself by writing it here...

_____

_____

_____

_____

_____

Use this space to draw a scene from the Bible or reflect on something you learned, felt or experienced...

113. What did David do after he attacked and captured the city of Rabbah?
(2 Samuel 12:27-31)

A. He built a temple for God in Rabbah
B. He built a house for his wife Bathsheba
C. He took the crown from the head of the King of Rabbah and placed it on his own head
D. He repented to the Lord for attacking the city of Rabbah

114. Why was David's son Amnon obsessed with his half-sister Tamar? (2 Samuel 13:1-2)

A. Because he claimed to love her and became obsessed with her
B. Because she was smarter than him
C. Because he enjoyed the food she cooked
D. Because he did not have a sister of his own

WEEK 9 MEMORY VERSE: JEREMIAH 32:27
I am the Lord, the God of all mankind. Is anything too hard for me?

115. What advice did Jonadab give Amnon about what to do about Tamar?
(2 Samuel 13:3-5)

A. "Invite her to teach you how to cook"
B. "Pretend to be sick so David will care for you himself"
C. "Go to bed and pretend to be sick, then ask Tamar to come and feed you"
D. "Throw Tamar into a pit so she can stop competing with you"

116. What did Amnon do to Tamar?
(2 Samuel 13:10-14)

A. He threw her into a pit in the middle of the night
B. He sold her as a slave to the Egyptians
C. He forced himself on her and hurt her deeply
D. He pretended to hate her food and made her upset

WEEK 9 MEMORY VERSE: JEREMIAH 32:27
I am the Lord, the God of all mankind. Is anything too hard for me?

117. What did Absalom do to Amnon?
(2 Samuel 13:28)

A. Absalom made Amnon his best friend

B. Absalom forced Amnon to marry Tamar

C. Absalom sold Amnon as a slave

D. Absalom told his men to kill Amnon

118. What did Shimei do to David?
(2 Samuel 16:5-7)

A. Shimei brought 200 donkeys with food for David

B. Shimei cursed and threw stones at David

C. Shimei married David's daughter Tamar

D. Shimei joined David's army to help him fight Absalom

WEEK 9 MEMORY VERSE: JEREMIAH 32:27
I am the Lord, the God of all mankind. Is anything too hard for me?

119. What advice did Ahithophel give Absalom to disrespect his father David?
(2 Samuel 16: 20-22)

A. He advised Absalom to destroy David's property

B. He told Absalom to curse his father in front of the people of Israel

C. He told Absalom to shame David by taking over his household, including sleeping with his concubines

D. He advised Absalom to burn down his father's house

120. What happened to Absalom as he was riding his mule? (2 Samuel 18:9)

A. His hair got caught in a tree and he was left hanging in mid-air

B. His mule saw an angel and refused to move forward

C. Absalom fell off the mule and died

D. Absalom froze and turned into a pillar of salt

WEEK 9 MEMORY VERSE: JEREMIAH 32:27
I am the Lord, the God of all mankind. Is anything too hard for me?

121. What did Joab and his men do to Absalom after they found him hanging in the tree?
(2 Samuel 18:14-17)

A. Joab ended Absalom's life, and his men helped bury him under a pile of stones

B. Joab gently helped him down and took him to King David

C. Joab tied him up and sent him away from Israel

D. Joab asked the people of Israel what they wanted to do with him

122. How did Barzillai help King David when he ran away from Absalom? **(2 Samuel 19:31-33)**

A. Barzillai was old and wealthy; he provided for David's needs

B. Barzillai agreed to have the Ark of God stay in his home

C. Barzillai helped to kill Absalom

D. Barzillai was a priest and prayed to God to help David

WEEK 9 MEMORY VERSE: JEREMIAH 32:27
I am the Lord, the God of all mankind. Is anything too hard for me?

123. **When a troublemaker called Sheba, son of Bikri, sounded the trumpet and shouted, what happened? (2 Samuel 20:1-2)**

A. The walls of Jericho fell down

B. All the men of Israel left David to follow Sheba, but the men of Judah stayed with David

C. The men of Judah ran away from David, but the men of Israel stayed with him

D. Bikri fell and died for dishonoring God

124. **How many concubines did King David leave to take care of his palace? (2 Samuel 20: 3)**

A. 1000

B. 5

C. 10

D. 500

WEEK 9 MEMORY VERSE: JEREMIAH 32:27
I am the Lord, the God of all mankind. Is anything too hard for me?

125. What weapon fell out of Joab when he stepped forward to meet Amasa?
(2 Samuel 20:8)

A. A stone
B. A spear
C. A dagger
D. An arrow

126. What happened when Joab met Amasa?
(2 Samuel 20:9-13)

A. Joab greeted him kindly, then attacked him without warning

B. Amasa was wounded, and people stopped when they saw him on the road

C. Joab's men moved Amasa's body so the army could continue their mission

D. All the above

WEEK 9 MEMORY VERSE: JEREMIAH 32:27
I am the Lord, the God of all mankind. Is anything too hard for me?

The Lord is my God,
and nothing is too hard for Him
(Jeremiah 32:27)

Great job completing the week!

**Did you memorize the daily verse?
Test yourself by writing it here...**

_____

_____

_____

_____

_____

_____

**Use this space to draw a scene from the Bible or reflect
on something you learned, felt or experienced...**

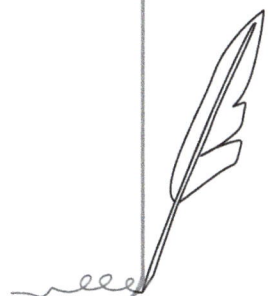

127. What happened after Amasa's body was moved out of the way? (2 Samuel 20:13)

A. The people of Israel became rebellious and wanted revenge

B. Everyone was able to move forward to pursue Sheba son of Bikri

C. The army of Amasa attacked the people of Gibeon

D. His family came to look for the body, but they could not find it

128. How did the wise woman of Abel save her city from destruction? (2 Samuel 20:15-22)

A. She told Joab not to destroy Abel because it was a peaceful city

B. She promised Joab the head of Sheba son of Bikri

C. She convinced the people to hand over Sheba

D. All the above

WEEK 10 MEMORY VERSE: 1 CHRONICLES 29:12

Both riches and honor come from You, and You reign over all. In Your hand is power and might; In Your hand it is to make great, And to give strength to all.

"

129. When David was King of Israel, what was Joab's job? (2 Samuel 20:23)

A. Joab was the King's best friend
B. Joab was the commander over Israel's entire army
C. Joab was the priest
D. Joab was a slave in David's palace

"

130. When David was King of Israel, what was Zadok and Abiathar's job? (2 Samuel 20:25)

A. They were slaves
B. They were David's armor-bearers
C. They were Priests
D. They were commanders of the army of Israel

WEEK 10 MEMORY VERSE: 1 CHRONICLES 29:12

Both riches and honor come from You, and You reign over all. In Your hand is power and might; In Your hand it is to make great, And to give strength to all.

"

131. Why was there a famine in Israel for 3 continuous years during David's reign? (2 Samuel 21:1)

A. Because Saul had killed the Gibeonites

B. The famine was caused by idol worship

C. There was no famine when David was king

D. The famine only lasted a short time

"

132. Were the Gibeonites part of Israel? (2 Samuel 21:2)

A. They asked for seven of Saul's descendants to be handed over to them for justice

B. They asked for David's daughter in marriage

C. They asked for the hill of Ephraim to be given to them

D. They asked for food and livestock for 7 years

WEEK 10 MEMORY VERSE: 1 CHRONICLES 29:12
Both riches and honor come from You, and You reign over all. In Your hand is power and might; In Your hand it is to make great, And to give strength to all.

"

133. What did the Gibeonites ask David to do for them? (2 Samuel 21:4-9)

A. They asked for seven of the male descendants of Saul to be killed

B. They asked for David's daughter in marriage

C. They asked for the hill of Ephraim to be given to them

D. They asked for food and supplies until the famine ended

"

134. What did Rizpah do when her sons were killed, and their bodies exposed on a hill? (2 Samuel 21: 8-10)

A. She protected the bodies from birds and wild animals day and night

B. She dropped a stone from a wall and killed the Gibeonite leader

C. She carried the bodies and buried them in Israel

D. She refused to eat for 40 days

WEEK 10 MEMORY VERSE: 1 CHRONICLES 29:12
Both riches and honor come from You, and You reign over all. In Your hand is power and might; In Your hand it is to make great, And to give strength to all.

135. In one of the battles with the descendants of Rapha, what did one of the men look like? (2 Samuel 21:20-21)

A. He was blind but very tall

B. He had very long hair

C. He was tall and blind but strong

D. He had six fingers on each hand and six toes on each foot

136. Read David's song of Praise to God in 2 Samuel Chapter 22. What did God do when David cried out for help? (2 Samuel 22:4)

A. David never cried to God

B. God heard David's cries and saved him from his enemies

C. God did not listen because David had killed people

D. God sent a rainbow in the sky

WEEK 10 MEMORY VERSE: 1 CHRONICLES 29:12
Both riches and honor come from You, and You reign over all. In Your hand is power and might; In Your hand it is to make great, And to give strength to all.

137. In David's last words, who spoke through him? (2 Samuel 23:1-2)

A. The prophet Samuel
B. David couldn't speak
C. David spoke for himself
D. The Spirit of the Lord

138. In David's last words, what did he say about a person who rules others in the fear of God? (2 Samuel 23:3-4)

A. That person is like the morning light on a clear day
B. That person is like brightness after rain that grows grass
C. All the above
D. None of the above

WEEK 10 MEMORY VERSE: 1 CHRONICLES 29:12

Both riches and honor come from You, and You reign over all. In Your hand is power and might; In Your hand it is to make great, And to give strength to all.

139. What did David do when three mighty warriors brought him water from the enemy's camp? (2 Samuel 23:15-17)

A. He thanked them and made them army leaders
B. He drank it and became sick
C. He refused to drink it and poured it out before the Lord
D. He shared it with the warriors

140. Which of the following things did Benaiah the mighty warrior do? (2 Samuel 23:20-21)

A. He chased a lion into a snowy pit and killed it, and defeated a huge Egyptian
B. Fought Philistines until his hand froze
C. Struck down two of Moab's strongest warriors
D. All the above

WEEK 10 MEMORY VERSE: 1 CHRONICLES 29:12
Both riches and honor come from You, and You reign over all. In Your hand is power and might; In Your hand it is to make great, And to give strength to all.

BONUS QUESTIONS

141. How long did it take to count all the fighting men in Israel? (2 Samuel 24:8)

A. 1 year and 3 months
B. 9 months and 20 days
C. 5 months and 15 days
D. 7 months

142. How many fighting men were counted in Israel and Judah? (2 Samuel 24:9)

A. 800,000 in Israel and 500,000 in Judah
B. 1 million total
C. 700,000 in Israel and 300,000 in Judah
D. 2 million total

WEEK 10 MEMORY VERSE: 1 CHRONICLES 29:12
Both riches and honor come from You, and You reign over all. In Your hand is power and might; In Your hand it is to make great, And to give strength to all.

BONUS QUESTIONS

143. Which punishment did David NOT have to choose from after he counted the people (2 Samuel 24:11-13)

A. 3 years of famine

B. 3 months fleeing from enemies

C. 3 days of plague

D. 3 years of oppression by foreign enemies

144. Which punishment did David choose after counting the people? (2 Samuel 24:12-15)

A. 3 years of famine

B. 3 months fleeing

C. 3 days of plague

D. 3 hours of natural disasters

WEEK 10 MEMORY VERSE: 1 CHRONICLES 29:12

Both riches and honor come from You, and You reign over all. In Your hand is power and might; In Your hand it is to make great, And to give strength to all.

BONUS QUESTIONS

145. Why did King David refuse to take Araunah's land and oxen for free? (2 Samuel 24:21-24)

A. Araunah was poor and had no other land

B. David did not want to offer God something that cost him nothing

C. David wanted to give to the poor

D. David feared the people would turn against him

146. How much did David pay for Araunah's oxen and threshing floor? (2 Samuel 24:24)

A. 500 Camels

B. 30 Shekels of gold

C. 50 shekels of silver

D. 100 Camels and 100 Goats

WEEK 10 MEMORY VERSE: 1 CHRONICLES 29:12
Both riches and honor come from You, and You reign over all. In Your hand is power and might; In Your hand it is to make great, And to give strength to all.

BONUS QUESTIONS

147. What did King David do with the land he bought during the plague? (2 Samuel 24: 24-25)

A. Built a burial place
B. Built an altar and offered sacrifices to the Lord
C. Asked the Lord to send fire from heaven
D. Gave it back to Araunah

148. What happened after David built an altar to the Lord and offered sacrifices? (2 Samuel 24:25)

A. The Lord answered his prayer, and the plague stopped
B. Fire came down and burned the altar
C. David became king over all nations
D. The people of Israel moved to a new land

WEEK 10 MEMORY VERSE: 1 CHRONICLES 29:12
Both riches and honor come from You, and You reign over all. In Your hand is power and might; In Your hand it is to make great, And to give strength to all.

The blessing of the Lord makes me rich, and He adds no sorrow with it.
(Proverbs 10:22)

Great job completing the week!

**Did you memorize the daily verse?
Test yourself by writing it here...**

_____

_____

_____

_____

_____

_____

**Use this space to draw a scene from the Bible or reflect
on something you learned, felt or experienced...**

Certificate of Completion

This Certificate Certifies That:

_____

Has Successfully Completed The
1st & 2nd Samuel Workbook!

Flo & Grace

_____
PARENT/TEACHER SIGNATURE

_____
PROJECT KINGDOM COME

WOULD YOU LIKE TO ACCEPT JESUS INTO YOUR HEART?

THE BIBLE SAYS:

If you confess with your mouth that Jesus is Lord and believe in your heart that God has raised Him from the dead, you will be saved
(Romans 10:9)

SAY THE PRAYER BELOW OUT LOUD AND BELIEVE IT IN YOUR HEART!

Dear Lord Jesus,
I know that I am a sinner, and I ask for Your forgiveness.
I believe You died for my sins and rose from the dead.
I repent of my sins and invite You to come into my heart and life.
I want to trust and follow You as my Lord and Savior. Help me to live
for you for the rest of my life.
I am now a child of God, and I ask You to fill me with Your Holy Spirit.

In Jesus' Name I pray, Amen.

Congratulations!
If you have prayed this prayer, please let an adult know or
send an email to mybibleworkbooks@gmail.com

ANSWER KEY:

1. C	13. D	25. B
2. B	14. B	26. A
3. A	15. D	27. C
4. D	16. C	28. C
5. A	17. B	29. D
6. D	18. A	30. B
7. C	19. C	31. D
8. A	20. D	32. A
9. A	21. A	33. C
10. B	22. A	34. B
11. D	23. C	35. B
12. C	24. B	36. C

ANSWER KEY:

37. D	49. D	61. C
38. B	50. A	62. B
39. D	51. D	63. C
40. B	52. C	64. D
41. C	53. A	65. A
42. A	54. A	66. D
43. C	55. B	67. B
44. C	56. C	68. C
45. A	57. D	69. B
46. B	58. D	70. D
47. B	59. B	71. C
48. C	60. A	72. D

ANSWER KEY:

73. B	87. A	100. D
74. D	88. C	101. C
75. C	89. C	102. A
76. C	90. A	103. B
77. D	91. B	104. C
78. C	92. A	105. D
79. B	93. D	106. C
80. D	94. B	107. B
81. C	95. A	108. A
82. C	96. D	109. C
83. B	97. D	110. D
84. C	98. C	111. A
85. D	99. B	112. A
86. A		

ANSWER KEY:

113. C
114. A
115. C
116. C
117. D
118. B
119. C
120. A
121. A
122. A
123. B
124. C
125. C

126. D
127. B
128. D
129. B
130. C
131. A
132. C
133. A
134. A
135. D
136. B
137. D
138. C

139. C
140. D
141. B
142. A
143. D
144. C
145. B
146. C
147. B
148. A

PLEASE GIVE US YOUR FEEDBACK!

Please send us your feedback on this workbook. We would love to hear what you enjoyed most, and ways you think it could be improved!

Please Send an email to: MyBibleWorkbooks@gmail.com, or leave us a comment on one of our social media pages.

✉ MyBibleWorkbooks@gmail.com

📷 Projectkingdomcome

f Projectkingdomcome

SCAN ME

> And I am certain that God, who began the good work within you, will continue His work until it is finally finished on the day when Christ Jesus returns.
>
> Philippians 1:6, NLT

DRAW HERE

DRAW HERE

DRAW HERE

DRAW HERE

www.ingramcontent.com/pod-product-compliance
Lightning Source LLC
Chambersburg PA
CBHW061409090426
42740CB00026B/3484